Why do BAD THINGS HAPPEN to GOOD PEOPLE?

David Arnold

CREATION
HOUSE

WHY DO BAD THINGS HAPPEN TO GOOD PEOPLE? by David Arnold
Published by Creation House
A Charisma Media Company
600 Rinehart Road
Lake Mary, Florida 32746
www.charismamedia.com

Unless otherwise noted, all Scripture quotations are taken from the *New King James Version* of the Bible. Copyright © 1979, 1980, 1982 by Thomas Nelson, Inc, publishers. Used by permission.

Scripture quotations marked TLB are from the *Living Bible*. Copyright © 1971. Used by permission of Tyndale House Publishers, Inc. Wheaton, IL 60189. All rights reserved.

Scripture quotations from *The Message: The Bible in Contemporary English* are used by permission of NavPress Publishing Group Copyright © 1993, 1994, 1995, 1996, 2000, 2001, 2002.

Scripture quotations from the *Amplified Bible* are used by permission of: the Zondervan Corporation, Old Testament copyright © 1965, 1987; the Lockman Foundation, New Testament Copyright © 1954, 1958, 1987.

Scripture quotations from *The Bible: James Moffatt Translation*, Copyright © 1922, 1924, 1925, 1926, 1935, Harper Collins San Francisco, CA Copyright 1950, 1952, 1953, 1954 James A. R. Moffatt. Used by Permission.

Word definitions are derived from the following sources: Scripture quotation from the Barclay translation is from *The Letter to the Romans*, third edition, by William Barclay, Louisville, KY: Westminster John Knox Press, 2002.

Strong, James. *Strong's Exhaustive Concordance of the Bible*, Nashville, TN: Royal Publishers, Copyright © 1973.

Earle, Ralph. *Word Meanings in the New Testament*. Peabody, MA: Hendrickson Publishers, Copyright © 1997.

Vine, W. E. *An Expository Dictionary of New Testament Words*. Westwood, NJ: Fleming H. Revell Company, Copyright © 1966.

Wuest, Kenneth S. *Wuest's Word Studies from the Greek New Testament*, Volumes 1,2,3. Grand Rapids, MI: W, B. Eerdman's Publishing Company, Copyright © 1973.

Novak, Alfons, *Hebrew Honey*, Houston, TX: Countryman Publishers, Copyright © 1987.

Library of Congress Control Number: 2008934069
International Standard Book Number: 978-1-59979-485-3
E-book ISBN: 978-1-59979-782-3
20 21 22 23 24 — 22 21 20 19 18
Printed in the United States of America

Contents

Dedication

This book is dedicated to my wife, Linda, who is my partner and encourager. I would also like to thank my family, and so many people whom I have served as a pastor. You helped influence much of what I have written in this book.

Introduction

Arthur Ashe was one of the most outstanding professional tennis players of all time. Not only was he a superb role model, but also a devoted husband and father. In 1979 and again in 1983, he endured two heart bypass operations. A few years later, he was diagnosed with AIDS. Arthur stated that he was sure he was infected with HIV through a blood transfusion. He had not found life to be easy, having to battle racism, a disease of the heart, and then, the malady of AIDS. When asked why, he answered, "It's one of the great moral questions. Why do bad things happen to good people? Because it's a matter of enduring them."[1]

King Solomon asked the same question. In Ecclesiastes 8:14, he said, "There is a strange thing happening here on the earth: Providence seems to treat some good men as though they were wicked, and some wicked men as though they were good. This is very vexing and troublesome" (TLB). According to this, sometimes the "good" suffer the evils that the wicked deserve, and the wicked prosper. Even Solomon admitted this is "troublesome." When we hear of a very wicked person facing tragedy, it is not quite so hard to make it fit in the scheme of life. But when a devoted person faces loss or heartache, it just simply does not make sense.

In Job 5:7, one of Job's "comforters," Eliphaz the Temanite, said, "Yet man is born unto trouble, as the sparks fly upward." Although his opinion as to why Job suffered was in error, in this statement he was correct. In all my years in the ministry, I've yet to meet one person who did not have problems, or some type of suffering. The old Spanish proverb is often in evidence: "There is no home in all the land which will not, sooner or later, have its 'Hush.'"[2]

It is my desire that in the pages of this book, I can give you some helpful answers to one of life's greatest enigmas—*why do bad things happen to good people?*

CHAPTER 1

The Shape of the World

*"Instead of creating a millennium,
we have contrived a madhouse."*[3]
VANCE HAVNER

A six-year-old boy was asked by his geography teacher about the shape of the world. He replied, "My dad says it's in awful shape." It is not being pessimistic, but realistic, to acknowledge this world is not in good shape. Violence, dishonesty, crime, disease, weather disasters, and immorality are rampant. Nations are in turmoil. The reason is because this world is cursed by sin, which we read about in Genesis. This helps us understand why bad things happen to good people.

An Imperfect World

When Albert Einstein was asked what he considered to be the most important question in the world, he replied, "Is the universe a friendly place?"[4] Of course, we all know the answer is a certain "no." This world is not a friendly place, but rather hostile.

The fact is, we live in an imperfect world, and we are all, good and evil, affected by it.

John stated in 1 John 5:19, "We know that we are of God, and the whole world lies under the sway of the wicked one." Sir Robert Watson-Watt was the Scotsman who invented the radar. While driving in Canada he was arrested for speeding—caught in his own radar trap. Later, he wrote this poem about his ordeal:

> *"Pity Sir Robert Watson-Watt,*
> *Strange target of his radar plot,*
> *And thus, with others I could mention,*
> *A victim of his own invention."*[5]

Sadly, we are all victims of our own invention, an imperfect world due to sin.

A man painted a picture of a boy with his satchel full of apples. He was hanging by the tips of his fingers from the top of a wall. Just above the wall on the other side was the owner of the orchard from which the boy had taken the apples. At the bottom of the wall was a big bulldog chained to a kennel. The boy could not go up for fear of the owner. He dared not drop down for fear of the dog. Below the picture were these words: "In A Fix."[6]

Romans 6:23 tells us, "The wages of sin is death." Sin is fatal, and we live in a world stained with sin. It is in quite "a fix."

A couple was vacationing in a remote mountain area. They stopped for some snacks at a grocery store. The woman who helped them had apparently not traveled far from her surroundings. The man's wife said, "I doubt she knows what's going on in the world outside."

Her husband responded, "Don't tell her. I don't want her to know. Let her live and die in peace."[7]

In John 16:33, Jesus said, "These things I have spoken to you, that in Me you may have peace. In the world you will have tribulation; but be of good cheer, I have overcome the world." This is both a word of assurance and a statement of fact. The assurance is that we can have inner peace in a tumultuous society, and we can overcome, instead of being overcome. However, the fact is, in this present world we will have tribulation, meaning, "anguish and trouble." This is why suffering touches the righteous as well as the unrighteous. In Matthew 5:45b, Jesus said, "He makes His sun rise on the evil and on the good, and sends rain on the just and on the unjust." He is revealing the Grace of God shown to all, whether deserving or undeserving. The same sun shines on all, and, whether evil or good, the benefits are the same.

When it rains, the rain does not differentiate between the evil and the good. Weather conditions make no distinctions. Along both the East coast and Gulf coast of the United States, there is the threat of hurricanes. These horrific storms make no distinction between Christians and unbelievers. When they come, they affect everyone. Why? Because we live together in a world that is not perfect, and it will never be perfect until Christ reigns.

Many years ago, a dike collapsed in Europe. Three million gallons of water escaped, draining the canal for seven miles. More than one million fish were killed, and a twenty-foot gorge was washed through a nearby field. It required sixty men using bulldozers for three weeks to move thirty thousand tons of soil and repair all the damage.

Later they discovered the reason for the dike's collapse—a little rat had burrowed through the embankment of a canal, and water began seeping through. Slowly, but surely, what began as a small trickle became a rushing stream. One bank then collapsed to a width of forty feet, and the water poured out in torrents. The financial cost was enormous. All begun by a small rodent.[8]

Likewise, had our first parents—Adam and Eve—only realized the enormous repercussions of their disobedience, they would have most likely reconsidered.

Ezekiel 18:4 warns, "The soul who sins shall die." The Hebrew word for *death* means "plague, destruction, and ruin." Arthur Pink wrote, "Read the annals of history, examine the reports of our police courts, study life in the slums of our large cities, and then ask, How come it, that man, the king of creation, designed and fitted to be its leader and lord, should have sunken lower than the animals? Illustrations are scarcely necessary to show how low man has sunk, for all who know vice as it really exists beneath the thin covering provided by the conventionalities of modern civilization, are only too painfully aware of the degradation and desolation which exist on all sides."[9]

In the Greek New Testament, there are several words for sin that bring further understanding of living in this present world. One is defined as "to miss the mark," meaning that we have fallen short of God's expectations for us. A second one presents a picture of a line on one side, and another line on the other side, that represents an area where it is illegal to be. We have stepped over the line into that which is illegal. The third suggests a slipping backward. It is like driving your car on an icy road; you hit a spot and the vehicle slips off the road. The word speaks of losing control of our lives, resulting in wrong behavior. A fourth one speaks of deliberate, willful sinning, knowing that what we do is wrong, but we do it anyway. Finally, the last means to incur a debt, much like creating an astronomical credit card debt, impossible to pay.

Francis Schaeffer observed, "Made in God's image, man was made to be great, he was made to be beautiful, and he was made to be creative in life and art. But his rebellion has led him into making himself into nothing but a machine."[10]

On the mountainsides of Colorado lie the ruins of

a mammoth tree. It stood for over four hundred years, surviving numerous lightning strikes and storms. It had resisted all of nature's blows, but now it lay rotting. What happened?

Small beetles had entered into that tree. They were beetles so small that any of us could have crushed them between our thumb and forefinger, yet they had brought down the giant of a tree.[11]

Sin started with an innocent look, but resulted in a worldwide plague. So, why do bad things happen to good people? One thing to consider is that we live in an imperfect world, stained with sin.

> *"Sin is, has been, and ever shall be*
> *the parent of misery."*[12]
> THOMAS CARLYLE

CHAPTER 2

The Normal Christian Life?

"Christianity is not an insurance policy against life's ills and troubles."[13]
BILLY GRAHAM

Two young Christians, whose nation was ruled by an atheistic, oppressive government, were released from prison. When asked, "What was it like, being persecuted for your faith?" They answered, "We thought it was the normal way for a Christian to be treated."[14] Sometimes bad things happen to good people because of their:

Godly Living

Paul told young Timothy, "Yes, and all who desire to live godly in Christ Jesus will suffer persecution" (2 Timothy 3:12). If we desire to do what is right and be faithful to Christ, difficulties will come. Many times, bad things happen, not because we have done something wrong, but because we are doing what is right! *The Message* Bible expresses it this way: "Anyone who wants to live all out for Christ is in for a lot of trouble. There's no getting around it."

Samuel Rutherford, the Scottish minister and theologian, said, "Through many afflictions we must enter into the kingdom of God…It is folly to think to steal to heaven with a whole skin."[15]

David obeyed God, yet had to hide in caves while fleeing for his life from King Saul. Paul committed his life completely to Christ, and found himself in prison. Peter even taught that we are not to be surprised when suffering comes, but to be surprised when it doesn't come. He said, "Beloved, do not think it strange concerning the fiery trial which is to try you, as though some strange thing happened to you" (1 Peter 4:12). The second word for strange Peter used means "unusual." Maybe this is why Philip Brooks said, "I do not pray for a lighter load, but for a stronger back."[16] He knew that righteous living would bring suffering and trouble.

Christ Jesus spoke very plainly about this in Matthew 5:11, 12. He said, "Blessed are you when they revile you and persecute you, and say all kinds of evil against you falsely for My sake. Rejoice and be exceedingly glad, for great is your reward in heaven; for so they persecuted the prophets who were before you." Notice, when speaking of difficulties coming, Jesus did not use the word *if*, but instead, *when*.

During a time of tremendous distress due to a crisis in his congregation, a godly pastor saw before him on the ground part of a torn newspaper. In it, he

8

read the words:

"No man is fully accepted until he has first been fully rejected."[17]

Few men suffered more than Paul. Right after his conversion, the Lord spoke to Ananias of him: "Go, for he is a chosen vessel of Mine to bear My name before Gentiles, kings, and the children of Israel. For I will show him how many things he must suffer for My name's sake" (Acts 9:11, 12). This certainly was the experience Paul had for his unwavering commitment to the Gospel. In 2 Corinthians 11:23–28, Paul listed the various hardships he endured. He spoke of being beaten numerous times, put in prison regularly, having his life threatened, being shipwrecked on the vast sea, facing the perils of robbers and his own countrymen, becoming weary, facing hunger and thirst, and dealing with problems in the churches. In Acts 14:22b, this same apostle stated, "We must through many tribulations enter the kingdom of God." The word *tribulations* means "persecutions" and "troubles." Paul had learned that bad things will happen simply because he loved God.

Notice with me a sampling of Scriptures concerning Christ and suffering: "He must suffer many things" (Luke 17:25); "It was necessary for Christ to suffer" (Luke 24:46); and "Christ had to suffer" (Acts 17:3). The Scriptures are also very plain when speaking of believers. Romans 8:17 speaks of "the sufferings of this present time." Philippians 1:29 states, "For to you it has been granted on behalf of Christ, not only to believe in Him, but also to suffer for His sake." Peter spoke of "suffering for righteousness sake" in 1 Peter 3:14, and of suffering "as a Christian" (1 Peter 4:16).

Charles Spurgeon said, "God does not put His servants in hothouses and rear them delicately, but He exposes them to trials that they may know how to bear it when it comes. The Lord will not screen you from those trials by which faith is strengthened."[18]

The renowned historian Arnold Toynbee once told of a problem faced by herring fisherman, off the coast of England. When they returned to the mainland to sell their fish, they placed them in tanks. Since the herring were not used to such confinement, they became sluggish, which gave their flesh an unpleasant taste. One of the fishermen, sensing the problem, placed a catfish in each of the tanks. Even though the catfish ate a few herring, their chasing of the herring kept them moving, and the herring arrived in good shape.[19] Likewise, God, at times, uses our sufferings, trials, and problems to keep us from getting spiritually slothful. Robert Schuller was correct when he wrote, "No problem leaves you where it found you." [20]

We can do one of three things when facing resistance: we can break out in rebellion against God; we can break down in despair; or, we can break through by overcoming and conquering.

The Bible records of Moses, "So the LORD spoke to Moses face to face, as a man speaks to his friend"

(Exodus 33:11), yet he too faced his difficulties while leading the people to the Promised Land. The Israelites constantly complained. Moses was criticized by his own brother and sister. He had to deal with the cowardice of the people concerning the giants in the land. There was a conspiracy against Moses, instigated by Korah, Dathan, and Abiram. Here was a man God spoke to "face to face, as a man speaks to his friend," yet he was not exempt from trouble.

Charles G. Finney said, "If you have much of the Spirit of God, it is not unlikely you will be thought deranged by many. You must make up your mind to this, and so much the more, as you live the more above the world, and walk with God."[21]

The book of Job deals with "the mystery of suffering." We know Job was a very godly man from the words of the opening chapter, verse one: "There was a man in the land of Uz, whose name was Job; and that man was blameless and upright, and one who feared God and shunned evil." Yet, he suffered tremendously, losing his children, business, and health. He was visited by those who arrived with their strong, personal opinions as to why this had happened. Eliphaz said that Job was suffering because he had sinned. Bildad was sure it was because he was a hypocrite. Zophar believed he was suffering the portion of a wicked man. Finally, Elihu, the youngest of the group, declared that Job needed an attitude adjustment, and must see all of this as the Lord's chastening. To be quite honest, their various opinions are sometimes correct, but, with Job's suffering, they were all wrong. I heard the finest summary of the story of Job from a veteran, godly minister. He said, "The story of Job is to teach us that there are those who do not have to be bribed to serve God." I suppose there is much about Job's experience we will never fully understand, but one thing we can know is this: one reason Job suffered is because he served God and Satan did not like it. David expressed, "Many are the *afflictions* [meaning "sorrow and trouble"] of the righteous, but the LORD delivers him out of them all" (Psalm 34:19). Remember, God only promises a safe landing, not a smooth ride.

Matthew Henry wrote, "Extraordinary afflictions are not always the punishment of extraordinary sins, but sometimes the trial of extraordinary graces."[22] A young couple went out as missionaries to India. They had served only a few years when the young husband was taken seriously ill. As the days and weeks passed, it became more apparent, outside of Divine intervention, he would not recover. His lovely, young wife could not bring herself to accept such disappointment and sorrow as a part of the will of God. Her grieved soul began to grow more rebellious and bitter. She cried to God for some sort of peace and an answer. But none came, until one day her husband called her to his side and said, "You know, my dear, we came over here to teach these people how to live as Christians and to show them the Christian way.

Now we are to have an opportunity to show them how Christians face things."

"As we get close to God, there are times of trial and testing. We can tell if we are clay or gold by how we respond. If we are clay, we become hard; if we are gold, we melt and flow with God's purpose."[23]

ANONYMOUS

Thou Shalt Not Smoke

"Keep your heart open to the correction of the
Lord, and be ready to receive God's chastisements,
regardless of who holds the whip."[24]
A. W. TOZER

I grew up in a home where neither alcohol, smoking, nor cursing were allowed. At thirteen years of age, my boyhood friend and I found several packages of cigarettes on the side of the road. Being typical, mischievous Southern boys, we decided to smoke, even though I knew fully well such things were forbidden by my parents. We climbed a large oak tree, no more than one hundred yards from my house, and began to puff away. However someone saw what we were doing and told my dad. A few minutes later, my father came along, and he was not in a pleasant mood. He looked up at us and asked if we were smoking. I answered him like any intelligent thirteen-year-old and said, "No, sir. We're not up here smoking."

He then ordered us both down, and approaching me, told me to breathe on him. That was my "death sentence." Dad told me to go to my room and wait for him. He then told my friend to go home and tell his parents what he had been doing. (I talked to this same friend over twenty-five years later, and he still had not told them.)

As I waited on my father, I knew this was not going to be good. Then my father entered the room. Now there are some people new to church life that think the laying on of hands is a recent practice. I can assure you it is not, because on that day, decades ago, my dad "laid hands on me," and when he departed, I was fully delivered from cigarettes!

Of course, I had disobeyed my father, and because of his love and concern for me, he could not allow this practice to continue. The lesson I learned was: Woe to the sibling who violated the Arnold's eleventh commandment, "Thou shall not smoke." This reveals another reason why bad things happen to good people:

Disobedience

A cantankerous church elder is reported to have told his pastor about his plans to visit the Holy Land. "As soon as I get to Mt. Sinai," he said, "I am going to run to the top, open my Bible, and read the Ten Commandments." Whereupon the pastor wisely advised, "Why don't you just stay home and keep them?"[25]

We need to consider that sometimes bad events are

16

God's chastening of us. Proverbs 3:11–12 says, "My son, despise not the chastening of the LORD, nor detest His correction. For whom the LORD loves He corrects, just as a father the son in whom he delights."

The word *chastening* means "discipline," from which we get the word "learner." Some of the most valuable lessons in life are learned through God's discipline. This is why we are not to reject or show contempt for it. The twelfth chapter of the book of Hebrews refers to these Scriptures in Proverbs, explaining that an earthly father, because of his love for his child, cannot allow him to walk in disobedience. The writer then admits that no correction is enjoyable, yet the result is "the peaceable fruit of righteousness to those who are trained by it" (12:11b).

John Bunyan tells us, "Afflictions are governed by God, both as to time, number, nature, and measure. Our times, and our conditions in these times, are in the hand of God, yea, and so are our souls and bodies, to be kept and preserved from the evil while the rod of God is upon us."[26]

Solomon said, "The foolishness of a man twists his way, and his heart frets against the LORD" (Proverbs 19:3). We knowingly disobey God, then blame either God or the devil for our predicament, when actually it was all our fault. Someone said, "Half our troubles come in wanting our way; the other half in getting it."[27]

God has established fixed laws of sowing and reaping. If we sow bad seed, we will get a bad result. The same is true with the law of gravity. If we cooperate, it is beneficial, but if we decide to defy this law and leap off a skyscraper, we reap fatal consequences.

We can bring either blessings or curses on our life, and the lives of others, by our actions. Proverbs 26:2 states clearly, "Like a flitting sparrow, like a flying swallow, so a curse without a cause shall not alight." A curse on a person's life is there due to a cause, an action on someone's part. Both the French and Italians have a proverb that states, "He who sows thorns, should not go barefoot,"[28] and an Arabian proverb says, "Curses are like young chickens, and they still come home to roost."[29]

Proverbs 3:33 teaches this truth: "The curse of the LORD is on the house of the wicked, but He blesses the home of the just." As a minister for many years, I have seen the fulfillment of this Scripture. Some have brought much heartache into their finances, family, marriage, etc., just because of not doing what was right. Yet others have had the blessings of God on them because of their obedient heart. Of course, no one earns God's favor. However, we can make certain decisions, and take specific actions, that place us either out of, or under, God's umbrella of blessings. Oswald Chambers reminds us, "The golden rule for understanding spiritual matters is not intellect, but obedience."[30]

God will use trouble to chastise us if need be. In Revelation 3:19, He said to the people of the Laodicean church, "As many as I love, I rebuke and chasten. Therefore be zealous and repent." The word for *love* means, "to have affection for," denoting "personal attachment, as a matter of sentiment or feeling." The word *rebuke* means "to admonish." *Chasten* means "to train up a child, educate, discipline by punishment, instruct, and teach."

Because God loves us, He will use difficulties to bring us to repentance, when we are not walking in obedience. It is through these situations we are instructed, and brought into a place of relationship with Him. As it has been so accurately stated, "God sends us the storms to prove that He is the only shelter."[31]

A lady was spending her summer in Switzerland. One day she went for a walk. As she ascended the mountainside, she arrived at a shepherd's fold, and saw a shepherd sitting with his sheep all around him. Close to him was a single sheep lying on a pile of straw. It seemed to be in pain. A closer look revealed that its leg was broken. With much sympathy, she questioned the shepherd as to what had happened. To her amazement, the shepherd answered, "Madam, I broke this sheep's leg."

Recognizing her astonishment, he continued, "Madam, of all the wayward sheep in my flock, this one was the most wayward. It would never obey my voice. It would never follow in the pathway in which I was leading the flock. It was constantly wandering away into dangerous situations, and was soon influencing the other sheep with its disobedience. I had experience in the past with this kind of behavior, so I broke its leg. The first day I tried to feed it, it tried to bite me. I allowed it to lie alone for a couple of days. Then, I went back to it. Now, it not only took the food, but licked my hand and showed every sign of submission, and even affection. When this sheep is well, it will be the model sheep of my flock. No sheep will be more obedient, and none will follow so closely at my side."[32]

The writer of Psalm 119 spoke of this lesson. In verse 67, he admitted, "Before I was afflicted I went astray, but now I keep Your word." The word *afflicted* means "humbled or disciplined," and speaks of any kind of trial. *Astray* speaks of departing from what is right. Through the temptations of life, carelessness, and negligence, he is saying he wandered off the right way and was going in a harmful direction. However, God allowed a trial to get his attention, and to lead him back on the right path. In verse 71, he says, "It is good for me that I have been afflicted, that I may learn your statutes." In verse 75, he further admits, "I know, O LORD, that Your judgments are right, and that in faithfulness You have afflicted me."

Dr. Richard Dobbins, in his book *Your Feelings: Friend or Foe*, writes, "At times, life deals potentially crippling blows to each of us. But what happens to us is not nearly as critical to our emotional and spiritual health as the way we choose to interpret and react to what happens."[33]

There is a legend about a grandfather clock that stood in a corner for three generations, faithfully ticking for years, months, weeks, days, hours, minutes, and seconds. Its means of operation was a heavy weight, suspended by a double chain. A new owner, believing that such an old clock should not have to bear such a heavy load, removed the weight, and immediately the clock stopped ticking.

The clock asked, "Why did you do that?"

The new owner answered, "I wanted to lighten your burden."

"Please put the weight back," requested the clock. "The weight is what keeps me going."[34]

All too often we try to escape the very things that will keep us going in the right direction. So much that contributes to our walk with God, and our character, are the weights of life. It is these that maintain our obedience.

"Grace grows better in the winter."[35]
CHARLES SPURGEON

CHAPTER 4

Echoes of Eternity

*"He who provides for this life, but takes no care for
eternity, is wise for a moment, but a fool forever."* [36]
TILLOTSON

Though most have never heard of him, Arthur Stace
of Sydney, Australia, was a unique individual.
After serving as a stretcher-bearer in World War I, he
became an alcoholic, and lived in abject poverty. In
1930, he received Jesus Christ as his Savior. Two years
later, he heard a minister speak on the subject "The
Echoes Of Eternity." He was so impacted by this
message about eternity, that he began to use his free
time to spread this one word message: Eternity.

With a piece of chalk, he wrote the word Eternity
on the sidewalks of Sydney, fifty times a day for over
thirty years,. Though he was confronted by the police
on twenty-three occasions, they never arrested him.
He died in 1967, at the age of 83. So popular had he
become, that the press, radio, and television reported
his passing. The day after his death, the morning
newspaper ran a front-page article headlined, "Mr.
Eternity Has Written His Last Word." [37]

It has been said, "The greatest business of life is to prepare for the next life." Another reason bad things can happen to good people, is that trouble seems to focus our lives on:

Eternal Things

In Colossians 3:1–2, Paul writes, "If then you were raised with Christ, seek those things which are above, where Christ is, sitting at the right hand of God. Set your mind on things above, not on things on the earth." Then, in the following verses, we are admonished to prepare for eternity. The word *affection* is defined, "to set one's mind on, be intent on." The same apostle reminded the church at Philippi, "For our citizenship is in heaven, from which we also eagerly wait for the Savior, the Lord Jesus Christ" (Philippians 3:20). James Moffatt translates the first part of this verse, "But we are a colony of heaven."[38] This is interesting since Philippi, to whose church this was written, was a Greek city far from Rome. However, it was in the Roman Empire, and a colony of Rome, in the sense that its citizens possessed Roman citizenship. The believers at Philippi recognized the authority of the emperor of Rome, and were to conduct themselves as Roman citizens, just as if they resided in Rome itself.

Paul is reminding the people at Philippi that, just as they constituted a colony of Rome on this earth, they were also a colony of heaven, so far as their heavenly citizenship was concerned. They were far from their true home and true Sovereign, the Lord Jesus Christ, in a wicked and perverse society. They were a heavenly people, with a heavenly citizenship, and a heavenly destination, and were to live heavenly lives in a foreign land. What was true of them is true of every believer in this age.

Matthew Henry wrote, "We are pilgrims and strangers, exiles and aliens, and this world is our passage, but not our portion."[39] Hebrews 11:13b refers to this truth by describing Christians as "strangers and pilgrims on earth," and Peter addresses the people of God as "sojourners and pilgrims" in this present world (1 Peter 2:11a). A pilgrim is a traveler, not a settler, keeping aware that material things are of value only as they help accomplish his purpose in this life. True pilgrims of faith look to the next world, because they know life is short and eternity is a reality.

Thomas Carlyle, the Scottish historian and essayist, said, "He who has no vision of eternity has no hold on time."[40] Certainly we are to remain faithful in this life, as Christ spoke of in Luke 19:13. However, while we have responsibilities in this life, we must also maintain a view of eternal life. "I'm tired of all this preaching about the hereafter," said one. "I'm living now, and I mean to have a good time. The hereafter isn't here yet." His companion said, "No, only the first part of it. But, I do wonder if the 'here' does not have a great deal to do with preparing for the 'after.'"[41]

In many respects, this is the message of the book of Ecclesiastes—a book of reality, not pessimism. The word *vanity* is frequently used, having the connotation of "chasing after soap bubbles." The message is: finding complete fulfillment in this life is as useless and frustrating as chasing soap bubbles. Solomon taught that the world's wisdom, pleasure, fame, wealth, etc., will never satisfy the human heart. Regarding this, Billy Graham stated, "Basically, he said, 'It's all just a bubble that bursts.'"[42] He sums it all up with, "Let us hear the conclusion of the whole matter: fear God and keep His commandments, for this is man's all. For God will bring every work into judgment, including every secret thing, whether good or evil" (Ecclesiastes 12:13,14).

A man related how he was once caught in a boat far from shore during a storm, and for one hour faced what seemed certain death. "It was strange (he said) how everything in my life changed value out there facing death. It was like looking through the other end of a telescope. Things I thought unimportant suddenly loomed large, and things I had deemed of first concern shriveled away ... Everything shifted in a hurry out there facing death and eternity."[43]

Martin Luther said that on his calendar there were only two days: "today" and "that Day."[44] In 2 Corinthians 4:18, we are told, "We do not look at the things which are seen, but at the things which are not seen. For the things which are seen are temporary, but

the things which are not seen are eternal." Someone
said, "When a dove begins to associate with a crow,
its feathers remain white, but its heart grows black."[45]
The influence of this world is powerful and attractive,
and this is why God uses difficulties and suffering to
drive us back into the reality of eternal things.

In Psalm 30:6, David confessed a natural tendency
in all of us. He said, "Now in my prosperity I said, 'I
shall never be moved.'" He is referring to some point
in his life when he had so many comforts that he began
to believe they could never be taken from him, giving
him a false sense of security. This shows the danger of
self-confidence, and makes us forget our dependence
on God. We become worldly-minded, and it becomes
necessary for God to teach us how easily it can all be
swept away. His purpose is to bring us back to a right
view of the uncertainty of all earthly things.

Certainly God wants to bless and prosper His
people, but not with the intent of causing us to forget
that we are aliens in this world. Someone reminds
us, "Christians sometimes feel that when prosperity
favors them, Satan is leaving them alone and God is
blessing them. It may be vice versa."[46]

The request of Agur, the son of Jakeh, in Proverbs
30:7–10, was, "Two things I request of You (deprive
me not before I die): remove falsehood and lies far
from me; give me neither poverty or riches—feed me
with the food allotted to me; lest I be full and deny
You, and say, 'Who is the LORD?' or lest I be poor

and steal, and profane the name of my God." He had enough concern to know that this world's abundance is not necessarily evil, but he could not allow it to steer him away from an eternal view of life.

Thomas Carlyle once stated, "Adversity is sometimes hard on a man; but for one man who can stand prosperity, there are a hundred that will stand adversity."[47] Adversity serves an eternal purpose if it refocuses us on things eternal.

"If I were lucky enough to call this entire estate mine, I would be a happy fellow," said a young man.

"And then?" questioned his friend.

"Why, then I'd pull down the old house, and build one much larger, have lots of friends around me, keep the best wines, and the finest horses and dogs in the country."

"And then?"

"Then I'd hunt, and ride, and smoke, and drink, and dance, and party, and enjoy life gloriously."

"And then?"

"Why then, I suppose, in the course of time, I would eventually die, and leave behind all these things."

"And then?"

"Oh, forget your 'thens,' I have to be on my way!"

Years later, the friend was met with a "God bless you! I owe my happiness to you!"

"How?"

"By two words spoken in season long ago—'And

then.'"[48]

"We were made for eternity as certainly as we are made for time; and as responsible moral beings, we must deal with both."[49]

A. W. TOZER

CHAPTER 5

Paid in Full by a Cold Glass of Milk

*"Shared joy is double joy,
and shared sorrow is half-sorrow."*
SWEDISH PROVERB[50]

A young man was working his way through medical school as an encyclopedia salesman. One hot, humid day—tired, weary, and discouraged—he approached a simple house. A young girl, about sixteen years of age, opened the door, and almost instantly sensed his physical and mental exhaustion. She gave him a cold glass of milk.

Years later, she was a patient in Johns Hopkins Hospital where the young man was now a lead surgeon. He immediately recognized her. When she received her bill, written across it was, "Paid in full by a cold glass of milk."[51]

A glass of milk had become a benevolent boomerang in the hands of a kind and compassionate country girl.

In his old age, pastor and evangelist Dr. F. B. Meyer

said that if he had his life to do over again, he would devote much more time to the ministry of comfort.[52] Sometimes bad things happen to develop a heart of:

Compassion and Comfort

In 2 Corinthians 1: 3–4, Paul stated, "Blessed be the God and Father of our Lord Jesus Christ, the Father of mercies and God of all comfort, who comforts us in all our tribulation, that we may be able to comfort those who are in any trouble, with the comfort with which we ourselves are comforted by God." When Paul and his companions were going through trouble and difficulties, God comforted them. Now, with the same comfort (Divine aid) God gave them, they were able to share with others. The message presented is: when suffering comes, we experience God's comfort. Then, when others are suffering, we can help them with the same compassion God gave to us.

I read on a sign years ago, "Medicine is a science, caring is an art." God wants us to be a caring, compassionate people, bringing comfort to our fellow man. A veteran minister stated, "There are sadder lives than yours in this world; go comfort them, and you will be comforted."[53]

Queen Victoria was a close friend of Principal and Mrs. Tulloch of St. Andrews. Prince Albert died and Victoria was left alone. At the same time, Principal Tulloch died and Mrs. Tulloch was left alone. Unannounced, Queen Victoria came to call on Mrs. Tulloch. She was resting on a couch in her room. When the queen was announced, Mrs. Tulloch struggled to rise quickly from the couch and curtsey. The queen stepped forward, and said to her, "My dear, don't rise. I am not coming to you today as the queen to a subject, but to another woman who has just lost her husband."[54]

In Colossians 4, Paul spoke of Tychicus, Onesimus, and Marcus. He said of them, "which have been a comfort to me" (v. 11). This word *comfort*, in the original Greek, is where we obtain our word "paregoric," a remedy that stops pain.[55] These men helped to stop the pain in Paul's heart.

The same was said of Titus. He never wrote a book, built a church, never worked miracles that we have record of, never preached a great sermon, as far as we know, and was certainly not a celebrity in the Kingdom. But, when Paul was at his lowest ebb, Titus came and encouraged him, lifted his spirits, and strengthened him for battles ahead. Note how Paul said it, "For indeed, when we came to Macedonia, our bodies had no rest, but we were troubled on every side. Outside were conflicts, inside were fears. Nevertheless, God, who comforts the downcast, comforted us by the coming of Titus" (2 Corinthians 7:5, 6). Could there be anything better to be said of us than was said of Titus?

God wants us to be a caring, compassionate people

in this cold, indifferent generation. Billy Graham wrote, "Another way we hurt people is by being too busy. Too busy to notice their needs. Too busy to drop that note of comfort, or encouragement, or assurance of love. Too busy to listen when someone needs to talk. Too busy to care."[56]

G. A. Studdard-Kennedy was a courageous British chaplain in World War I. He said if any person was undisturbed by the pain and suffering of others, that person was suffering either from "hardening of the heart, or softening of the brain!"[57]

Jeremiah spoke of the way God cared for him during a most devastating event in his life. In Lamentations 3:55–57, he said, "I called on Your name, O Lord, from the lowest pit. You have heard my voice: 'Do not hide Your ear from my sighing, from my cry for help.' You drew near on the day I called on You, and said, 'Do not fear!'"

Notice that he declared that God did not "hide" His ear when he needed someone to listen. The word for *hide* speaks of "un-neighborliness, people who turn their eyes away from a needy situation." God never turns His eyes nor ears away from us when we need Him. We are to do the same for others.

Abraham Lincoln said, "I feel sorry for the man who can't feel the whip when it is laid on another man's back."[58] When the whip of troubles, problems, and difficulties are laid on our back, and we experience the comfort and compassion of God, this should be a learning experience for us to be more sensitive toward others when they encounter the same.

Have you had tragic loss? If so, you can not only sympathize with others facing the same suffering, but can empathize also. Have you fallen from grace, only to have the loving hand of God bring you to complete restoration? You, then, are to give that same hand of love and compassion to other fallen people. It is so easy to be harsh and judgmental of others, until you face the harsh realities of life yourself. Have you been abandoned, and found the Lord to be your best Friend? Then, do the same for others.

The prophet Jeremiah spoke of those who have "pain, but do not profit" (Jeremiah 12:13b). He is saying that some do not learn any valuable lessons about life, and the heart of God, through their bad experiences. God wants us to profit from our pain, by growing more comforting and compassionate toward our fellow man. Learn to give to others, who are going through difficulties and tragedy, the same understanding and grace that God gave you.

Mother Teresa once explained, "Love has a hem to her garment that reaches the very dust. It sweeps the streets and the lanes, and because it can, it must."[59]

Years ago in the deep South, late at night, an older African-American woman was standing on the side of a road, trying to endure a violent thunderstorm. Her car had broken down, and she desperately needed a ride. Her clothes became soaking wet, as she unsuccessfully tried to get someone to stop. Then, an almost unheard of thing, in those days of racial conflict, happened.

A young white man stopped, took her to safety, assisted her, and paid for her taxi ride. As she profusely thanked him, she took the time to write down his name and address. Several days later, there was a large console television delivered to the young man's home. A special note was attached that read: "Thank you so much for assisting me on the highway that dark and dangerous night. That storm drenched not only my clothes, but my spirit as well. Then you stopped and so compassionately helped me. Because of you, I was able to make it to my dying husband's bedside just before he died. God bless you for helping me, and unselfishly serving others. Sincerely, Mrs. Nat King Cole."[60]

> *"You may forget with whom you laughed, but you will never forget with whom you wept."*[61]
> ARAB PROVERB

CHAPTER 6

I Want to Be Like God

*"In Christian service the branches that bear
the most fruit hang the lowest."*[62]
ANONYMOUS

A man applied for a job, and the company told him the only opening they had was down in the mail room. He took it, thinking, "Well, I do need a job, so I'll take it." On his first day at work, he looked over and saw a cockroach. He said to himself, "I'll kill the roach, and show them I'm working hard."

As he approached, the cockroach said, "Wait a minute. If you won't kill me, I'll give you anything you want."

Of course, the man was surprised, and said, "Okay, I want to be company president by tomorrow."

The cockroach snapped his fingers and declared, "You've got it."

The next day the man went to work, and to his astonishment, they made him president of the company. As he was sitting at his desk, enjoying all the power and influence, he looked over and saw the same cockroach running across the floor. He said to the cockroach, "I want to be chairman of the board."

The roach said, "Sure," snapped his fingers again, and promised, "Tomorrow, you'll be chairman of the board."

The following day, when he arrived, he was informed that he was now chairman of the board. As he was sitting in his big chair behind his large desk, he heard a noise above him. Going to investigate, he found a young boy on the roof, praying. He asked the boy what he was doing, and the lad said, "I'm talking to God."

The man went back down to his elegant office. The same cockroach appeared, stating, "If you promise not to kill me, I'll give you anything you wish."

The man told the roach, "Listen, I want to be like God."

The cockroach said, "You got it."

The next morning, when the man showed up for work, he was back in the mail room![63]

Another reason why bad things happen to good people, is because through these experiences, God deals with our pride and develops more humility in us.

Pride and Humility

In 2 Corinthians 12:7–10, Paul admitted, "And lest I should be exalted above measure by the abundance of revelations, a thorn in the flesh was given to me, a messenger of Satan to buffet me, lest I be exalted above measure. Concerning this thing I pleaded with the Lord three times that it might depart from me. And He said to me, 'My grace is sufficient for you, for My strength is made perfect in weakness.' Therefore most gladly I will rather boast in my infirmities, that the power of God may rest upon me. Therefore, I take pleasure in infirmities, in reproaches, in needs, in persecutions, in distresses, for Christ's sake. For when I am weak, then I am strong."

Paul was being honest enough to confess that he could very easily become infected with a spirit of pride. Therefore, God used trouble and difficulty to keep him in touch with his humanity.

Someone said, "Conceit is the devil's gift to little men."[64] It is sad to watch someone begin with dependence on God, then, when a little success comes their way, they become so filled with pride and self-importance they "strut even while sitting down." Because God is watching over us, He will allow suffering, disappointment, and failure to come to bring us back to the reality of our humanness. Alan Redpath, in his book *Blessings Out of Buffetings*, wrote that the word for *thorn,* that Paul used in 2 Corinthians 12:7, does not mean a kind of thorn we might get in our finger while doing yard work.[65] The meaning of thorn, as Paul used it, is a "stake upon which people were impaled to be crucified." Therefore, Paul spoke of very severe trials that worked in him dependency on, and humility before, God. He knew how deceitful this spirit of pride and self-importance is, and no one is exempt. Many a person has been brought low, after exalting themselves, when God gave them some measure of success.

John Bunyan once preached an especially powerful sermon. The first person he spoke to afterward told him so. He said, "Yes, I know. The devil told me that as soon as I walked away from the pulpit."[66]

The Bible declares that there are "six things the LORD hates, and seven that are an abomination to Him" (Proverbs 6:16, 17). "A proud look" is at the top of the list. By placing "pride" as number one, does this mean that pride is worse than lying, murder, and the other terrible things listed? Let us never forget that it was pride, and an inflated opinion of himself, that caused Satan's fall from heaven. Someone stated, "Religious pride is dangerous! It can blind individuals to their own faults, and it can reinforce their prejudices. Whenever persons begin to note their remarkable spiritual progress, they are in great danger!"[67]

Proverbs 11:2 reminds us, "When pride comes, then comes shame; but with the humble is wisdom." Also, Proverbs 29:23 says, "A man's pride will bring him low, but the humble spirit will retain honor." If the need arises, God will let trouble and suffering come to us. He foresees the shame and humiliation awaiting us because of our feelings of self-importance. These seemingly bitter experiences may actually be our salvation from destruction. Proverbs 16:18, 19 confirms this: "Pride goes before destruction, and a haughty spirit before a fall. Better to be of a humble spirit with the lowly, than to divide the spoil with the proud."

Dwight L. Moody, the great American evangelist of the nineteenth century, was not a man of formal education. His letters were full of grammatical errors. He was unimpressive in his physical appearance. His voice was high-pitched and his tones nasal. But these things did not hinder God from using him to reach two continents with the gospel. A reporter was sent to cover Moody's campaigns in Britain in which aristocrat and artisan alike turned to God. The reporter's purpose was to discover the secret of Moody's influence and power. After lengthy observation, he wrote, "I can see nothing whatever in Moody to account for his marvelous work." When Mr. Moody read the article, he chuckled, "Why, that is the very secret of the movement. There is nothing in it that can explain it, but the power of God. The work is God's, not mine."[68]

It is interesting to discover that the word *humus*, the decayed vegetable matter that plants draw their nourishment from, comes from the same root that gives rise to the word "humility." It is through the humiliating experiences in life, the kind that leave "mud on our face," that fertile soil is created from which something new and fresh can grow. Peter Marshall, one-time chaplain of the U. S. Senate, rose rapidly to success in his ministry. He also served as Senior Pastor of one of the most prestigious churches in Washington, D.C. He suffered a heart attack that left him incapacitated for a while. In the fall of 1946, when he had resumed his work again, a minister friend came to visit him, and asked, "Well, Peter, I'm curious to know something. What did you learn during your illness?" Peter Marshall answered promptly, "Do you really want to know? I learned that the Kingdom of God goes on without Peter Marshall."[69]

We can tell when a believer is growing, in proportion to his growth in grace. He elevates his Master, talks less of what he is doing, and becomes smaller and smaller in his own esteem, until, like the morning star, he fades away before the rising sun. In the Louvre, in Paris, there is a famous painting by Murillo, entitled, *The Miracle of San Diego*. The painting depicts a scene in which a door opens, and two noblemen and a priest enter the kitchen. They are amazed to find that all the kitchen maids are angels. One is handling a water-pot, another a piece of meat, a third a basket of vegetables, a fourth is tending the fire. There are at least two messages here. One is that no service is common unless we make it so. The second is that, by patient toil and humility, we develop the qualities that are celestial.[70]

*"Do you wish to be great? Then, begin by being.
Do you desire to construct a vast and lofty fabric?
Think first about the foundations of humility.
The higher your structure is to be,
the deeper must be its foundation."*[71]
AUGUSTINE

42

CHAPTER 7

A Greek Scholar and An Old Saint

"It is better to walk in the dark with God than to go it alone in the light."[72]

ANONYMOUS

A Bible scholar and professor tried to explain to a dear old saint of a lady that Hebrews 13:5b could actually be read, "I will never, never, never leave you nor forsake you." The old saint replied, "The Lord may have to say it three times to get you Greek scholars to believe it, but once is enough for me!" [73]

Difficulties Strengthen Our Faith and Trust in God

Charles Spurgeon reassured his congregation, "He cannot lie, He never will revoke His word. Has He said, and shall He not do it? He has spontaneously made the promise, and He will divinely make it good. Upon every promise, the blood of Jesus Christ has set its seal, making it 'yea and amen' forever."[74]

The writer of Hebrews 13:5b—"For He Himself

has said, '*I will never leave you nor forsake you*'"
(emphasis added)—had also learned this to be true.
The words, "He Himself has said," are very intensive
in the Greek, telling us that the Lord Jesus Christ
Himself has made this promise. The word *leave* means
"to uphold," or "sustain." The promise is, "I will not, I
will not cease to uphold or sustain you." *Forsake* means
that the Lord will not let us down in a state of defeat
or helplessness while we are going through hostile
circumstances. A dear saint expressed, "Suffering is
not always sent to burn out the dross; sometimes it is
meant to burn in the promises."[75] Difficulties, trials,
problems, and yes, even sufferings, can teach us that
God is dependable, if we allow them to.

David Livingstone, the legendary medical
missionary to Africa, returned to his homeland of
Scotland. He was the recipient of the degree of Doctor
of Law at the University of Glasgow. As he stood
before the audience to speak, his body showed all too
clearly the signs of exposure, physical hardships, and of
more than thirty attacks of tropical fever. His left arm
hung useless at his side, the result of being attacked by
a lion. The students and faculty were moved to tears, as
he told of his experiences and the announcement of his
soon coming return to Africa. "But, I return," he said,
"without misgiving, and with gladness of heart. Shall
I tell you what has sustained me during all this time of
labor, suffering, and difficulty in the villages of dark
Africa, among people whose attitude toward me was

always uncertain and often hostile? It was the promise of Christ, 'Lo, I am with you always, even to the end of the world'. On those words I staked everything, and they never failed. I was never left alone."[76]

The Psalmist testified, "And those who know Your name will put their trust in You; for You, LORD, have not forsaken those who seek You" (Psalm 9:10). When he spoke of "Your name," he was not speaking of a proper name, but of the character of God. It is one thing to know and recite one of the names for God in the Bible, but it is quite another to learn of the character and integrity of God. The word *trust* means "to become acquainted with." It is through bad times that we can become better acquainted with God. Corrie Ten Boom, a Holocaust survivor, said, "When the train goes through the tunnel, and it gets dark, you don't throw away the ticket and jump off. You sit still and trust the engineer."[77]

Martin Luther was in the middle of the Reformation, and the Pope was trying to bring him back into the Catholic church. A cardinal was sent to persuade Luther back with gold. The cardinal wrote back to the Pope, "The fool does not love gold." Luther was then threatened with the statement, "Do you think the Pope cares for the opinions of a German boor? The Pope's little finger is stronger than all of Germany. Do you expect your princes to take up arms to defend you—you, a wretched worm like you? I tell you no. And where will you be then?" Luther's reply was simple: "Where I am now. In the hands of Almighty God."[78]

We are admonished in Psalm 37:3 to, "Trust in the LORD, and do good; dwell in the land, and feed on His faithfulness." The word *trust* means "to place one's hope in, to go to for refuge, and to have confidence in." Faith and trust in God grows and develops as we face both good and bad in life. It is not difficult to trust God when things are fine, but the real test comes when life is difficult. This is when we decide, or not, to put our confidence and hope in God. When we do, we discover Him to be faithful once again.

As a young, single woman, Lillian Thrasher journeyed to Egypt, and soon thereafter God placed on her heart the plight of the multitudes of homeless children. In 1911, she opened an orphanage with nothing but her faith in God. Over the next fifty-one years, she faced many challenges, difficulties, disappointments, and, yes, victories. Today, there still stands the Lillian Thrasher Memorial Orphanage. Her motto always was, "O God, since You enabled me to do the simple things that I could do, I have full trust in You to do the great things which I cannot do."[79]

The Bible is full of admonishments to put our trust in God. Psalm 2:12b states, "Blessed are all those who put their trust in Him." Psalm 34:8 tells us, "Oh, taste and see that the LORD is good; blessed is the man who trusts in Him." Again, Psalm 62:8 reads, "Trust in Him at all times, you people; pour out your heart before Him; God is a refuge for us. Selah." And the two middle verses of the Bible are, "It is better to trust in the Lord than to put confidence in man. It is better to trust in the Lord than to put confidence in princes" (Psalm 118:8–9).

Billy Bray was gloriously saved from the bondage of sin, and then gave his life in service to Christ. Concerning his faith and trust in God, he once said, "If Billy gets work, he praises the Lord; when he gets none, he sings all the time. Do you think that He'll starve Billy? No, no, there's sure to be a bit of flour in the bottom of the barrel for Billy. I can trust in Jesus, and while I trust Him, He'd soon starve Michael the Archangel as He'd starve Billy."[80]

Proverbs 3:5–6 admonishes, "Trust in the LORD with all your heart, and lean not on your own understanding; in all your ways acknowledge Him, and He shall direct your paths." Here we are told four vital truths about trust: we are to trust in the Lord *diligently*, "Trust in the LORD with all your heart;" we are to trust in the Lord *submissively*, "And lean not on your own understanding;" we are to trust in the Lord *completely*, "In all your ways acknowledge Him;" and we are to trust in the Lord *expectantly*, "He shall direct your paths."

Chuck Swindoll said, "If finding God's way in the suddenness of storms makes our faith grow broad, then trusting God's wisdom in the daily-ness of living makes it grow deep."[81]

A young English curate set out on a sunny afternoon in the spring for a walk. His path led him through a limestone gorge about two and one half miles long. As he was enjoying the exercise and scenery, he did not notice the storm clouds gathering overhead. Finally, he did look up, and seeing the dark, overcast sky, he turned and ran for home. However, the storm overtook him. The rain descended in torrents, and the young curate found cover in a cleft of a great limestone rock. As he stood there in the place of shelter, and heard the thunder roar, and saw the lightning flash, he was deeply moved. He drew from his pocket a pencil and a scrap of paper, and wrote:

> *"Rock of Ages, cleft for me,*
> *Let me hide myself in Thee."*

This was the inspiration that led Augustus M. Toplady to write one of the world's greatest hymns.[82]

> *"When you have nothing left but God,*
> *you begin to learn that God is enough."*[83]
> ANONYMOUS

CHAPTER 8

Keep Swingin' at 'Em

*"Great works are performed not by strength,
but by perseverance."*[84]
SAMUEL JOHNSON

Few people know that Babe Ruth struck out 1,330 times during his baseball career. Yes, he did eventually hit 714 home runs, but he also missed, and missed, and missed the ball. But, what people remember about Babe Ruth is his 714 home runs, a record unparalleled for decades.

Someone asked Ruth the secret of his success at the plate. He replied, "I just keep goin' up there, and keep swingin' at 'em."[85]

Disappointments and adversity teach us:

Perseverance

James wrote, "My brethren, count it all joy when you fall into various temptations, knowing that the testing of your faith produces patience. But let patience have its perfect work, that you may be perfect and complete, lacking nothing" (James 1:2–4). The word *all* speaks of the totality of things—not just one experience, but all the experiences of life. The word *patience* means "endurance" and "perseverance." The words *perfect and complete* speak of maturity and a well-balanced life.

James is telling us that God uses the totality of our experiences to teach us perseverance, to mature us into a well-balanced person. Peter said, "In this you greatly rejoice, though now for a little while, if need be, you have been grieved by various trials, that the genuineness of your faith, being much more precious than gold that perishes, though it is tested by fire, may be found to praise, honor, and glory at the revelation of Jesus Christ" (1 Peter 1:6–7). If we will persevere, even in difficult times, the result will be a stronger faith and an eternal reward.

William and Katherine Booth were both known for their tenacity. She experienced bad health throughout her life, and both battled against an entire culture of oppression. In 1912, years after the death of his wife, Mr. Booth was having severe trouble with his eyes. His surgeons told him he must be operated on quickly. Standing before ten thousand parishioners in London's Royal Albert Hall, he stated, "I am now going into dry dock for repairs." On May 23, facing his second surgery, he was noticeably cheerful. In his study, he dictated several letters and signed documents. However, two days after this surgery, he was told infection had set in and that he would never see again.

He asked, "You mean that I am blind?"

The answer was, "Yes."

After a long pause, Mr. Booth declared, "God must know best." He then squeezed his son's hand, and said, "I have done what I could for God with my eyes. Now I will do what I can for God and the people without my eyes."

Even though he died three months later, he once again demonstrated his tenacity while facing disappointment and difficulty.[86]

It is very easy to serve God when things are going well, however, it is quite another thing to persevere in bad times. Anyone can give when there is an abundance of money. It takes perseverance to do so when finances are slim. Prayer is no problem when answers are evident on a daily basis. It is quite another experience to pray and pray, day after day, with no sign of an answer. Booker T. Washington stated, "Success is not measured by the heights one attains, but by the obstacles one overcomes in their attainment."[87]

In 2 Corinthians 1:24b, Paul wrote, "For by faith you stand." One of the most important lessons to be learned in military training is to stand well. Experienced soldiers know there is nothing that can test the courage, and the obedience of men, as to be required to hold their position in the face of the enemy. Some of the greatest victories have been won on the battlefield by men who refused to surrender against insurmountable odds. Arthur W. Pink, in his superb three-volume *Exposition of the Gospel of John,* wrote of Christ's disciples, "Like young recruits, they had yet to learn that it is one thing to know the soldier's drill and wear the uniform, and another to be steadfast in the day of battle."[88]

James J. Corbett, the champion prizefighter of years ago, said this about winning: "When your feet are so tired that you have to shuffle back to the center of the ring, fight one more round. When your arms are so tired that you can hardly lift your guard, fight one more round. When you wish your opponent would put you to sleep, fight one more round. The man who fights one more round is never whipped."[89]

The story of Nehemiah's mission to rebuild the wall of Jerusalem is a story of perseverance. In chapter four, we find that when the wall was half-finished, the enemy intensified their efforts to stop the work. The people were growing discouraged and considering giving up. However, Nehemiah rallied the people with four vital truths: he said to *remember*: "Remember, the Lord, great and awesome" (v. 14); *rebuild*: "All of us returned to the wall, everyone to his work" (v. 15); *rally*: "Whenever you hear the sound of the trumpet, rally to us there. Our God will fight for us" (v. 20); and *resist*: "The men held the spears from daybreak until the stars appeared" (v. 21).

When the days are dark, remember who God is, and that He will fight for you. Rebuild, keep doing what is right and pleasing to God, and remain faithful.

Allow your heart to rally by listening to His voice and meditating on the promises of His Word. Then, fight on, resist, keep believing against the false propaganda of the devil. Emerson said, "What lies behind us, and what lies before us, are tiny matters compared to what lies within us."[90]

In 1 Corinthians 1:9, Paul reminds us, "God is faithful." Then, fourteen chapters later, he admonishes: "Therefore, my beloved brethren, be steadfast, immovable, always abounding in the work of the Lord, knowing that your labor is not in vain in the Lord" (15:58). Apart from his greetings, this is the end of his letter, and it seems as though Paul connects this verse with the one in the first chapter. He is saying, "God is faithful .... therefore be steadfast, immovable." How can we persevere? Because God is faithful! Louis Pasteur said, "Let me tell you the secret that has led me to my goal. My strength lies solely in my tenacity."[91]

People who have accomplished much for God, and their fellow man, have not always been those who were the most gifted or intelligent. Many had to overcome great odds against them. Thomas Edison's teachers told him he was too stupid to learn. As a boy, Lou Gehrig was asked to quit the team because he was such a poor baseball player. As a young man, Walt Disney was told he had no good ideas. Beethoven was deaf as he composed most of his famous music. Mozart was told by his publisher that he would never get any money for his music. The author of *Little Women*, Louisa May Alcott, was told by an editor that she should stick to sewing, because she had no writing ability. Homer, the poet, was blind, as was Fanny Crosby, the writer of some of our most inspirational hymns. Woodrow Wilson, the twenty-eighth president of the United States, did not learn to read until he was ten.[92] Hebrews 11 gives many other examples of those who persevered against all odds.

In 1940, Charley Boswell signed a contract with a professional baseball team, and was on his way to a successful career. Then came World War II. One morning, in a small German town, an enemy anti-tank gun not only shattered his tank, but also his eyes and his dreams. Professional baseball has no place for a blind man. During his recovery, a young corporal, Kenny Gleason, at Valley Forge, Pennsylvania, invited him out for a game of golf. Charley had never played golf before. He thought Kenney was just kidding or crazy! But the young corporal persisted, and Charley agreed. Kenny spent a few minutes explaining the game, then lined Charley up at the practice tee and told him to swing. The ball went 200 yards straight down the fairway. Eventually, Charley Boswell played in at least thirty-nine national and international blind golf tournaments, winning twenty-eight of them. He also built a successful insurance business, while serving on a number of civic and physical-fitness committees. In 1971, he was appointed Revenue Commissioner of

Alabama. Charley said, "You can see why I consider blindness not a handicap, but an inconvenience."[93]

"I thought when I became a Christian I had nothing to do but lay my oars in the bottom of the boat and float along. But I soon found that I would have to go against the current."[94]
D. L. MOODY

CHAPTER 9

Invaded by the Boll Weevil

"The difficulties of life are intended to make us better, not bitter."[95]
ANONYMOUS

In 1915, Coffee County, Alabama, was facing devastation. They had been invaded by the boll weevil, destroying their cotton-growing industry. In the midst of this hopelessness and despair, the scientist, George Washington Carver, advised them to turn from growing cotton to peanuts. Through his research on the peanut, he had discovered unbelievable wealth with such products as shampoo, ink, paper, soap, plastics, and a host of other valuable uses. Listening to his advice, they made the change, and prosperity returned. In 1919, the people of Coffee County built a memorial to the boll weevil with the words: "In profound appreciation of the boll weevil and of what it has done as the herald of prosperity, this monument is erected by the citizens of Enterprise, Coffee County, Alabama."[96] What was thought to surely be a curse, turned into a blessing.

It is so easy in life to perceive things with the

wrong perspective. This is why, when bad things happen, they remind us again that:

Perception Is Stronger Than Truth

The way people perceive something may be totally opposite of reality, but to them, it is the truth. So often, our perspective on suffering and difficulty is mistaken. Corrie Ten Boom said it best: "Picture a piece of embroidery placed between you and God, with the right side up toward God. Man sees the loose, frayed ends; but God sees the pattern."[97]

In Romans 8:28, we have some of the most popular words ever written, "And we know that all things work together for good to those who love God, to those who are the called according to His purpose." This is a promise to those who love God and walk in obedience to Him.

First, we are told that things happen for our assurance, for it is "ALL THINGS." *All things* is exactly what it says—the good and the bad. If we really believe that God loves us, we believe that He is involved in every detail of our lives. Psalm 37:23 declares, "The steps of a good man are ordered by the Lord, and He delights in his way." The *Amplified Bible* states it this way: "The steps of a [good] man are directed and established by the Lord, when He delights in his way, and [He busies Himself with his every step.]"

Rowland V. Bingham founded the Sudan Interior Mission. He was a man who strongly believed in the guidance and goodness of God. He was seriously injured in an automobile collision in his sixtieth year. His head was severely cut, and a number of bones were broken. When he gained consciousness on the following day in the hospital, he asked the nurse why he was there.

"Be very quiet," she replied, "for you have been in a terrible accident."

"Accident, accident!" exclaimed Bingham. "There are no accidents in the life of a Christian. This is an incident!"[98]

Second, things happen as a matter of guidance for "all things WORK." An old Italian proverb says, "When God shuts a door, He opens a window." Many have come to barriers in their life, only to discover that these meant new and broader opportunities. In Genesis 42:36, during a time of much trouble and suffering, Jacob cried, "All these things are against me." In reality, all things were working for his family to be restored and protected. His perception was stronger than the truth.

George Mueller once said, "God not only orders the 'steps' of a good man, but also his 'stops.'"[99] A young man was accepted for the African mission field. He reported to New York to set sail, but found through further inquiry that his wife could not stand the climate. He was discouraged and heartbroken, and he returned home. Eventually, he became determined to make all the money he could to be used in spreading the message of Christ all over the world. His father, a dentist, had started to make unfermented wine on the side to be used for communion services. The young man took the business over, and developed it into a major enterprise. His name was "Welch," and his family still manufactures "grape juice."[100] Mega amounts of dollars have been given to the work of missions by this corporation.

> *"I learn as the years roll onward,*
> *And leave the past behind,*
> *That much I have counted sorrow*
> *But proves that my Lord was kind;*
> *That many a flower I longed for*
> *Had a hidden thorn of pain;*
> *And many a rocky bypath*
> *Led to fields of golden grain."*[101]

Third, things happen for our benefit, "For we know that all things work together FOR GOOD." It seems to be a mockery to say that all things are good. Disease is not good. The death of loved ones and friends is not good. Injury, drug addiction, divorce, etc., are not good. But the promise is that God takes all things and makes them work together for good. A chemist takes chemicals, that individually would be fatal to humans, and mixes them together so they serve

60

as medicine to bring healing. Table salt is composed of chloride and sodium, both of which are deadly poisons if consumed separately. However, mix them properly and we have table salt. The proper amount of salt intake is needed, because we cannot live without some salt in our systems.

The Barclay translation assures, "We know that God inter-mingles all things for good for them that love Him." Sir James Thornhill painted the cupola (a rounded roof or ceiling) of that world-famous structure, St. Paul's Cathedral in London. He had to work as he stood on a swinging scaffold high above the ground. One day, when he had finished a detail on which he had spent days of painstaking effort, he stopped and began to study his work. He became lost in thought. As he stood gazing at the structure, he began to move slowly backward in order to get a better view, forgetting where he was. A man who was with him became suddenly aware that one more backward step would mean a fatal fall for Thornhill. With his own brush, quick as a flash, he made a sweeping stroke across the picture. The distracted artist stopped, and rushed forward protesting loudly with anguish and anger. But when his companion explained his strange action, the great artist burst into expressions of gratitude.[102] Someday, we will thank God for some of our losses and disrupted plans.

*"God is able to let you rise from bed every morning
of the week with that blessed thought directly or
indirectly: 'I am in God's charge.
My God is working out my life for me.'"*[103]
ANDREW MURRAY

CHAPTER 10

Mrs. Einstein

*"The dealings of the Father's hand must ever be
looked at in the light of the Father's heart."* [104]
ARTHUR W. PINK

Someone once asked Mrs. Einstein whether she understood Professor Albert Einstein's Theory of Relativity. She said, "No, I don't understand the Theory of Relativity, but I know my husband, and I know I can trust him."[105] Bad things happen to teach us that eventually we must focus on, not what happened, but on:

Who God Is

A. W. Tozer warned, "Nothing twists and deforms the soul more than a low or unworthy conception of God."[106] There is a small Eastern European town of 4,000 with an alarming suicide rate. The newspaper ran this headline: "Suicide Stalks Isolated Village." Residents here commit suicide in every conceivable way. One man tossed himself into an abandoned well. Some overdose on drugs, others cut their wrists, drink poison, and even leap in front of trains. Entire families have taken their lives, from the young to the aged. The town is a desolate, lonely community, one hundred miles south of Budapest. A doctor, who operates a psychiatric clinic, told a reporter, "Some people call the road here the 'narrow road to the cursed place'... it is ingrained in the people that God doesn't like us very much."[107]

John wrote, "God is love" (1 John 4:16). John Wesley stated, "This little sentence brought St. John more sweetness, even in the time he was writing it, than the whole world can bring. God is often styled holy, righteous, wise; but not holiness, righteousness, or wisdom in the abstract, as he said to be love; intimating that this is his darling, his reigning attribute, the attribute that sheds an amiable glory on all his other perfections."[108]

The apostle Paul wrote these words to the believers in Ephesus: "That Christ may dwell in your hearts through faith; that you, being rooted and grounded in love, may be able to comprehend with all the saints what is the width and length and depth and height—to know the love of Christ which surpasses all knowledge; that you may be filled with all the fullness of God" (Ephesians 3:17–19). *Rooted and grounded* means "to build under a deep and stable foundation of knowing and understanding the love of God to you." *Comprehend* here suggests "to eagerly seize or lay hold of." The knowledge of God's love to us is the foundational truth upon which all other truths are built. We are to seize this truth, and make it the foundation of our walk with God. He adds that this love of God *surpasses knowledge,* meaning "experiential knowledge." No matter how much we experience the love of Christ, there are yet oceans of love in the heart of God.

In his book *I Shall Not Want*, Robert Ketchum tells of a Sunday school teacher who asked her group of children if anyone could quote the entire 23rd Psalm. A cute little blonde girl, age four and a half, was among those who raised their hands. The skeptical teacher asked her if she really could quote the entire psalm. The little girl came to the front of the room, faced the class, made a perky little bow, and said, "The Lord is my Shepherd, that's all I want." She bowed again and sat down. The teacher thought to herself that this may well have been the greatest interpretation of the 23rd Psalm ever heard![109]

When Paul spoke of the *width, length, depth,* and *height* of God's love, he was drawing upon the imagery of a large building. This, no doubt, reminded the Ephesian residents of the huge temple of Artemis located in the city. When J. T. Wood excavated it, he found that it rested on a platform 418 feet long by 239 feet wide, that was reached by a flight of ten steps. Three more steps led up into the sanctuary surrounded by towering pillars, rising up to the height of a five-story building. Yet, declared Paul, this paled in comparison to the love of God.[110]

Among the many victims of the Paris Commune was a Catholic bishop. He was a man who knew something of the love of God. In the small cell, where he was waiting execution, was a small window in the shape of a cross. After his death, there was found written above the cross, "height," below it, "depth," and at the end of each arm of the cross, "length" and "breadth." His message was that God's love is unfailing, even in the hour of adversity and death.[111]

> *"His love no end or measure knows,*
> *No change can turn its course;*
> *Eternally the same it flows*
> *From one eternal Source."*[112]

King Hezekiah, after recovering from his sickness, wrote, "Indeed it was for my own peace that I had great bitterness; but You have lovingly delivered my soul from the pit of corruption, for You have cast all my sins behind Your back" (Isaiah 38:17). The Hebrew word for *lovingly* means "to join," or "fasten together." God's love fastens to us like glue! It also means "to attach with warm affection," meaning that God loves us with warm affection. Further, it means "to delight in doing, to please." God delights in His people, and wants to give us the desires of our heart.

A short time before he died, Adolph Monod, the famous evangelical French preacher, commented, "I have strength for nothing more than to think about the love of God. He has loved us—that is the whole of dogmatics; let us love Him—that is the sum-total of the ethics of the Gospel."[113]

In Luke, chapter 15, Christ gave three parables, speaking of a lost coin, a lost sheep, and a lost son. These three parables are not simply three ways of presenting the same truth. They differ. The coin was lost through no fault of its own. Many an innocent person has suffered at the hands of another. The sheep was lost due to foolishness. There are those who would have never made some choices, if they had realized the consequences. The son deliberately became lost, callously turning his back on his father. Each one was found and redeemed. The love of God can restore the lives of the innocent, defeat the foolishness of man, and overcome even the rebellion of the heart.

When Isaac Watts was just a boy, he lived next door to an elderly Christian lady who took a special interest in him. He sensed her love for him, so he often visited her. One day, she noticed how enthralled Isaac was with a Scripture motto on her wall. The passage came from Genesis 16:13. It was Hagar's prayer, as she was put out of Abraham's house. The short motto simply read, "Thou God seest me."

Because of his interest in it, the old lady decided to give Isaac the motto. As she took it down from the wall and handed it to him, she said, "Son, I want you to have this. When you get older, you'll meet people who will want to make you believe that this Scripture means God is following you with a judgmental eye, watching everywhere you go, seeing everything you do, searching for some reason to judge you. Don't you believe them! For what this passage really means is that God loves you so much that He just cannot take His eyes off of you!"[114]

*"God does not love you because you are important,
you are important because God loves you."*[115]
ANONYMOUS

Conclusion

"Until a man has found God,
and been found by God, he begins at no beginning,
and he works to no end."[116]
HERBERT G. WELLS

In Deuteronomy 33:27, Moses reminded the children of Israel, "The eternal God is your refuge, and underneath are the everlasting arms." *Eternal* means "to go before, or precede, to be in front." God is in front, and after, all things and all creatures. We must remind ourselves not to be afraid of the future because He is our future.

The Eternal God
"Before the hills appeared,
Or rivers and the seas,
Before the clouds were formed
To ride on gentle breeze;
Before a man was born,
Or any living thing;
Before the rain or snow
Or flowers in the spring;

> *And ere the paths of earth*
> *By mortal men were trod:*
> *Before it all, there was*
> *The great eternal God.*
> *When everything on earth*
> *Decays and disappears,*
> *As darkness of the night*
> *Dissolves when daylight nears;*
> *When stars no longer shine*
> *And heavens pass away;*
> *When time shall be no more—*
> *No longer night and day;*
> *When skeptics and agnostics*
> *Are all beneath the sod,*
> *And none are left to challenge—*
> *There still will be our God!"*[117]

> *"Our unknown future is safe in the hands of*
> *the all-knowing God."*[118]
> ANONYMOUS

70

About the Author

David Arnold holds a Bachelor of Arts Degree in Bible, and a Master's Degree in Theology. He has been in the ministry, serving as an evangelist and pastor, since 1970, and is presently senior pastor of Gulf Coast Worship Center, New Port Richey, Florida.

He and his wife, Linda, have three children, and several grandchildren. His weekly articles, "60 Seconds," are syndicated worldwide, via the internet. He also writes a monthly article for a local Tampa Bay, Florida, area newspaper.

He is the author of *Discipleship Manual*.

To order additional copies of *Why Do Bad Things Happen to Good People?* visit:

www.davidarnoldonline.org
or phone toll free
(866) 396-READ
davidarnold1@verizon.net

Endnotes

Introduction

1 Jenkins, Sally. "Another Battle Joined" *Sports Illustrated*, April 20, 1992, p. 24.

2 Truett, George W. D.D., *Follow Thou Me*, Harper Brothers Publishers, New York and London, Copyright© 1932, p. 48.

Chapter 1: The Shape of the World

3 Havner, Vance, *Hearts Afire*, Fleming H. Revell Co., Old Tappan, New Jersey, Copyright © MCMLII, p. 85.

4 www.borysenko.powersource3.com/tapebook/044670154.cfm

5 www.microwaves101.com/encyclopedia/roughjustice.cfm

6 *The Teen–Age Teacher*, Edited and Published by Gospel Publishing House, Springfield, Mo., Volume XXIII, April, May, June, 1954, No. 2, p. 4.

7 Havner, Vance, *Just A Preacher*, Moody Press, Chicago, 1981 by The Moody Bible Institute of Chicago, p. 29.

8 *Robert G. Lee's Sourcebook Of 500 Illustrations*, Copyright ©1964 by Zondervan Publishing Co., Grand Rapids, Michigan, p. 186.

9 Pink, Arthur W., *Gleanings in Genesis*, Moody Press, Copyright ©1922 by The Moody Bible Institute of Chicago, p. 47.

10 *Pulpit Helps*, Chattanooga, Tennessee, AMG International, December 2001.

11 http://www.fosterroadchurch.org/messageofweekhtm

12 Jones, E. Stanley, *The Unshakable Kingdom and the Unchanging Person*, p. 48.

Chapter 2: The Normal Christian Life?

13 Graham, Billy, *Till Armageddon – A Perspective on Suffering*, Word Press, Waco, Texas, Copyright© 1981, p. 66.

14 Ibid. p. 107

15 Ibid. p. 115

16 Ibid. p. 121

17 Sanders, J. Oswald, *Robust In the Faith*, Moody Press, Copyright ©1965, p. 116

18 www.gracegems.org/15/sweet_affliction.htm

19 *Pulpit Helps*, Chattanooga, Tennessee, AMG International, May, 2004

20 Schuller, Robert H., *Move Ahead With Possibility Thinking*, Family Library, Doubleday and Co., Copyright ©1967, p. 97

21 www.gospeltruth.net/1868lect_on-Rev_of_ Rel/68revLec07.htm

22 J Wallace Hamilton, Ride the Wild Horses (Westmont, NJ: Fleming H. Revell Co., 1952).

23 *Pulpit Helps*, Chattanooga, Tennessee, AMG International, December, 1997.

Chapter 3: Thou Shalt Not Smoke

24 www.etherzone.com/2008/cron032108.shtml

25 *Adult Teacher Supplement*, Third Quarter, Gospel Publishing House, Springfield, Mo. 65802, Copyright ©1968, p. 5.

26 Graham, Billy. *Till Armageddon – A Perspective On Suffering* Word Press, Waco, Texas, Copyright 1981, p. 158.

27 *Pulpit Helps*, Chattanooga, Tennessee, AMG International, August 1998.

28 www.giga-usa.com/quotes/topics/proverbs_t382.htm

29 www.worldofquotes.cm/author/Proverb/58/index.
    html

30 The Pentecostal Evangel, April, 15, 2001.

31 *Pulpit Helps*, Chattanooga, Tennessee, AMG
    International, September, 2004.

32 Walter B. Knight, Knight's Master Book of New
    Illustrations (Grand Rapids, MI: Wm. B. Erdmans,
    1956), 642.

33 Dobbins, Dr. Richard D. *Your Feelings: Friend Or
    Foe*, Copyright ©2003 by Richard D. Dobbins, p. 33

34 Hamilton, J. Wallace. *Ride The Wild Horses* Fleming
    H. Revell Company, Westwood, N. J., Copyright
    ©MCMLII, p. 149

35 Drummond, Lewis A. *Love: The Greatest Thing in
    the World*, Copyright ©1998, Kregel Publications, p.
    101.

Chapter 4: Echoes of Eternity

36 www.giga-usa.com/quotes/authors/john_tillotson_
    a0001.htm

37 *Live* magazine, Gospel Publishing House, Springfield,
    Mo. January 13, 1974.

38 Moffatt, James A. R. *The Bible: James Moffatt
    Translation*, Copyright © 1922, 1924, 1925, 1926, 1935,
    Harper Collins San Francisco, CA Copyright 1950,
    1952, 1953, 1954 Used by Permission.

39 *The Best Of Vance Havner*, Fleming H. Revell, Old
    Tappan, New Jersey, Pyramid Publications, Inc., 1937,
    p. 111.

40 www.thetruelight.net

41   Knight, Walter B. *Knight's Master Book of New Illustrations*, Wm. B. Eerdmans Publishing Company, Grand Rapids, Michigan, Copyright ©1956, p. 284.

42   *Decision* magazine, June 2008, p. 2.

43   Havner, Vance. *It Is Time*, Fleming H. Revell, Old Tappan, New Jersey, Copyright ©MCMXLIII, pp. 90–91.

44   Dayton, Howard. *Ministry Insights* Crown Financial Ministries, Money Matters, 601 Broad Street SE, Gainesville, Ga. 30501, October 2002, Issue 297, p. 16.

45   www.creativeproverbs.com/cgi-bin/sql_search3cp.cgi?boolean=and&field=all&keyword=black

46   *Pulpit Helps*, Chattanooga, Tennessee, AMG International, October 1997, Old Union Reminder.

47   www.worldofquotes.com/topic/adversity/index.html

48   *The Adult Teacher*, Gospel Publishing House, Springfield, Mo. Jan., Feb., March, 1940, pp. 59, 60.

49   www.scribd.com/doc/2452829/knowledge-of-The-Holy-by-A-W-Tozer

Chapter 5: Paid in Full by a Cold Glass of Milk

50   www.cybernation.com/quotationcenter/quoteshow.php?id=33785

51   *Christian Clippings*, August, 1997.

52   Sanders, J. Oswald. *Robust In the Faith*, Moody Press, Chicago, Illinois, Copyright © 1965, p. 149.

53   *Live* magazine "Evangelist Stanley P. MacPherson" Gospel Publishing House, Springfield, Mo.

54   Barclay, William. *The Gospel Of Matthew, Volume One*, Chapters 1 to 10, The Westminster Press, Philadelphia, Pa., Copyright © 1975, p. 105.

55 Knight, Walter B. *Knight's Master Book of New Illustrations*, Wm. B. Eerdmans Publishing Company, Grand Rapids, Michigan, Copyright ©1956, p. 356.

56 Graham, Billy. *Till Armageddon – A Perspective On Suffering* Word Press, Waco, Texas, Copyright ©1981, p. 186.

57 Dennison, A. Dudley, M. D. Shock *It To Me Doctor* Zondervan Publishing Co., Grand Rapids, Mich., 1970, p. 88.

58 www.2.newpaltz.edu/WritingBoard/newsletter/reflecting.htm

59 *Impart Magazine* publication of Rick Renner Ministries, Tulsa, Ok, August, 2007, p. 5.

60 *Christian Clippings*, August, 2001.

61 www.nepab.com/general/quotes.htm

Chapter 6: I Want to be Like God

62 www.theoldtimegospel.org/dev/quote10.html

63 Chuck Swindoll, Esther: *A Woman of Strength and Dignity* (Nashville, TN: Thomas Nelson, 1997) story credited to Dr. Robert R. Koop.

64 Pentz, Croft M. *The Complete Book Of Zingers*, Tyndale House Publishers, Inc. Copyright © 1990, p. 252.

65 *Blessings Out Of Buffetings* Fleming H. Revell, Old Tappan, New Jersey, Copyright ©MCMLXV, p. 214

66 www.jewels4god.org/chapter9AngelsintoDemons.html

67 *Pulpit Helps*, February, 1998.

68 Sanders, J. Oswald, *Robust In the Faith*, Moody Press, Copyright ©1965, p. 100.

69 Marshall, Catherine. *A Man Called Peter, The Story*

Of Peter Marshall McGraw-Hill Book Company, Inc. New York, N.Y., Copyright ©MCMLI, pp. 233–234.

70 *Christian Clippings*, September, 2007. pp. 12 and 13.

71 www.cognitivedistortion.
com/?cd=quotes&search=Humility

Chapter 7: A Greek Scholar and an Old Saint

72 *Christian Clippings*, December, 1996

73 "Havner, Vance. *Hearts Afire* Fleming H. Revell, Old Tappan, New Jersey, Copyright ©MCMLII, p. 159.

74 Spurgeon, Charles Haddon. *Revival Sermons* Zondervan Publishing House, Grand Rapids, Michigan,1958, p. 84.

75 *Live* magazine. Gospel Publishing House, Springfield, Mo. December 2, 1973.

76 www.wayoflife.org/fbns/david-livingstone-pathfinder.
html

77 www.brainyquote.com/quotes/authors/c/corrie_ten_
boom.html

78 Knight, Walter B. *Knight's Master Book of New Illustrations*, Wm. B. Eerdmans Publishing Company, Grand Rapids, Michigan, Copyright ©1956, p. 19.

79 *Letters From Lillian* Assemblies of God Division of Foreign Missions, Springfield, Mo., Copyright ©1983, p. 125.

80 Ludwig, Charles. *Mother Of An Army* Bethany House Publishers, Minneapolis, Minnesota, Copyright ©1987, p. 164.

81 Swindoll, Charles R. *Devotions For Growing Strong In The Seasons Of Life*, Zondervan Publishing House, Copyright 1983, p. 321.

82 Knight, Walter B. *Knight's Master Book of New*

Illustrations, Wm. B. Eerdmans Publishing Company, Grand Rapids, Michigan, Copyright ©1956, pp. 140–150.

83 www.e-steeple.com/browse-by- topic/s/satisfaction. html

Chapter 8: Keep Swingin' at 'Em

84 www.wordtothewall.com/content/view/39/177/

85 www.rogerswebsite.com/articles/The-Truth-Shall-Set-You-Free.htm

86 Ludwig, Charles. *Mother Of An Army* Bethany House Publishers, Minneapolis, Minnesota, Copyright ©1987p. 230.

87 *Adult Teacher Supplement*, Gospel Publishing House, Springfield, Mo., 1965, p. 37.

88 Pink, Arthur W. *Exposition Of The Gospel Of John*, Volume Three, Zondervan Publishing House, Grand Rapids, Mich. Copyright 1945, pp. 84 – 85.

89 www.skyferret.blogspot.com

90 www.quoteworld.org/quotes/4458

91 www.umsl.edu/commencement/speakers/clear.htm

92 *Christian Clippings*, September 1995.

93 *Readers Digest*, November, 1971.

94 *Christian Clippings*, February, 2008, p. 22.

Chapter 9: Invaded by the Boll Weevil

95 www.quotegarden.com/hang-in.html

96 Hamilton, J. Wallace. *Ride The Wild Horses* Fleming H. Revell Company, Westwood, N. J., Copyright ©MCMLII, p. 152.

97 www.jerryengland.blogspot.com/2003_07_01_archive.

html

98 Knight, Walter B. *Knight's Master Book of New Illustrations*, Wm. B. Eerdmans Publishing Company, Grand Rapids, Michigan, Copyright ©1956, pp. 582 583.

99 *Adult Teacher Supplement*, Gospel Publishing House, Springfield, Mo. Third Quarter, 1966, p. 10.

100 Knight, Walter B. *Knight's Master Book of New Illustrations*, Wm. B. Eerdmans Publishing Company, Grand Rapids, Michigan, Copyright ©1956, p. 580.

101 Ibid. pp. 581 – 582

102 Ibid p. 581

103 www.wordinvisible.com/library/murray/ absolutesurrender/abssur5.html

Chapter 10: Mrs. Einstein

104 Pink, Arthur W. *Exposition Of The Gospel Of John Volume Two* Zondervan Publishing House, Grand Rapids, Mich. Copyright ©1945, p. 164.

105 www.thinkexist.com/quotation/no_i_don't_ understand_my_husband-s_theory_of/205395.html

106 www.crossroad.to/Excerpts/books/faith/Tozer/tozer-faith.htm

107 Wilkerson, David. "A Place Called Wit's End," *Times Square Church Pulpit Series*, April 4, 1995, p. 4.

108 *Adult Teacher Supplement*, Third Quarter, Gospel Publishing House, Springfield, Mo. 1969, p. 61.

109 *Christian Clippings*, April, 2004.

110 *Adult Teacher Supplement*, First Quarter, Gospel Publishing House, Springfield, Mo. 1971, p. 12.

111 Moody, D. L. *Anecdotes, Incidents And Illustrations*,

Morgan & S, 1898, p. 67.

112 *Exposition Of The Gospel Of John Volume Two* Zondervan Publishing House, Grand Rapids, Mich. Copyright ©1945 p. 296.

113 *Adult Teacher Supplement*, Gospel Publishing House, Fourth Quarter, 1966, p. 54.

114 www.whiteestate.org/sop/2000/sermon.html/

115 www.mywholeworldischanging.blogspot. com/2008/02/proverbs-quotes-whatever-ponder.html

Conclusion

116 Zubko, Andy. *Treasury Of Spiritual Wisdom: A Collection Of 10,000 Quotations* Matilal Banarsidass Publisher Copyright ©1996, p. 189.

117 Watkins, Grace V. "The Eternal God Grace" *Evangel* Magazine, Gospel Publishing House, Springfield, Mo, July 15, 1973.

118 www.rbc.org/devotionals/our-daily-bread/2002/06/24/ devotion.aspx